D0248540

TO..

FROM..

WINE GIVES
COURAGE AND
MAKES MEN
MORE APT
FOR PASSION.

OVID

IT'S
ALWAYS
WINE
O'CLOCK

summersdale

IT'S ALWAYS WINE O'CLOCK

First published in 2014
This edition copyright © Summersdale Publishers Ltd, 2017

Images © Shutterstock

Summersdale Publishers Ltd
46 West Street
Chichester
West Sussex
PO19 1RP
UK

www.summersdale.com

Printed and bound in the Czech Republic

ISBN: 978-1-78685-007-2

Substantial discounts on bulk quantities of Summersdale
books are available to corporations, professional associations
and other organisations. For details contact general
enquiries: telephone: +44 (0) 1243 771107 or email:
enquiries@summersdale.com.

WINE

IS ONE OF THE MOST
CIVILISED THINGS IN
THE WORLD.

ERNEST HEMINGWAY

ARTISTS AND POETS STILL FIND LIFE'S MEANING IN A GLASS OF WINE.

JOY STERLING

SOBRIETY DIMINISHES,
DISCRIMINATES, AND
SAYS NO; DRUNKENNESS
EXPANDS, UNITES AND
SAYS YES.

WILLIAM JAMES

HERE'S TO THE CORKSCREW – A USEFUL KEY TO UNLOCK THE STOREHOUSE OF WIT, THE TREASURY OF LAUGHTER, THE FRONT DOOR OF FELLOWSHIP, AND THE GATE OF PLEASANT FOLLY.

W. E. P. FRENCH

WINE
IS
LIFE.

PETRONIUS

AH, DRINK AGAIN
THIS RIVER THAT
IS THE TAKER-
AWAY OF PAIN,
AND THE GIVER-
BACK OF
BEAUTY!

EDNA ST. VINCENT MILLAY

CHAMPAGNE IS APPROPRIATE FOR BREAKFAST, LUNCH OR DINNER.

MADELINE PUCKETTE

EVERYBODY'S GOT
TO BELIEVE IN
SOMETHING. I
BELIEVE I'LL HAVE
ANOTHER DRINK.

PETER DE VRIES

A WALTZ AND
A GLASS OF
WINE INVITE
AN ENCORE.

JOHANN STRAUSS

NO ANIMAL
EVER
INVENTED
ANYTHING
SO BAD AS
DRUNKEN-
NESS – OR
SO GOOD
AS DRINK.

G. K. CHESTERTON

LIKE HUMAN
BEINGS, A WINE'S
TASTE IS GOING
TO DEPEND A
GREAT DEAL ON
ITS ORIGINS AND
ITS UPBRINGING.

LINDA JOHNSON-BELL

I COOK
WITH WINE,
SOMETIMES
I EVEN ADD
IT TO THE

food.

W. C. FIELDS

ALCOHOL IS NOT

THE ANSWER;

IT JUST MAKES YOU

FORGET THE QUESTION.

ANONYMOUS

WHENEVER

— *a man is* —

TIRED,

wine

IS A GREAT

restorer

OF STRENGTH.

HOMER

I ONLY TAKE A
DRINK ON TWO
OCCASIONS –
WHEN I'M THIRSTY
AND WHEN I'M NOT.

BRENDAN BEHAN

A MAN WILL
BE ELOQUENT IF
YOU GIVE HIM
GOOD WINE.

RALPH WALDO EMERSON

THE SOFT EXTRACTIVE
NOTE OF AN AGED CORK
BEING WITHDRAWN HAS
THE TRUE SOUND OF A MAN
OPENING HIS HEART.

WILLIAM S. BENWELL

NOW IS THE
TIME FOR DRINKING,
NOW THE TIME TO
DANCE FOOTLOOSE
UPON THE EARTH.

HORACE

WHITE WINE IS LIKE
ELECTRICITY. RED WINE
LOOKS AND TASTES LIKE A
LIQUEFIED BEEFSTEAK.

JAMES JOYCE

TOO MUCH
CHABLIS
CAN MAKE
YOU WHABLIS.

OGDEN NASH

FERMENTATION

EQUALS CIVILISATION.

JOHN CIARDI

WINE IS BOTTLED POETRY.

ROBERT LOUIS STEVENSON

TEETOTALLERS LACK
THE SYMPATHY AND
GENEROSITY OF MEN
THAT DRINK.

W. H. DAVIES

WINE IS A
PASSPORT
TO THE WORLD.

THOM ELKJER

CHAMPAGNE IS ONE OF THE ELEGANT EXTRAS IN LIFE.

CHARLES DICKENS

A HANGOVER IS
THE WRATH OF
GRAPES.

DOROTHY PARKER

A BOTTLE OF WINE CONTAINS MORE PHILOSOPHY THAN ALL THE BOOKS IN THE WORLD.

LOUIS PASTEUR

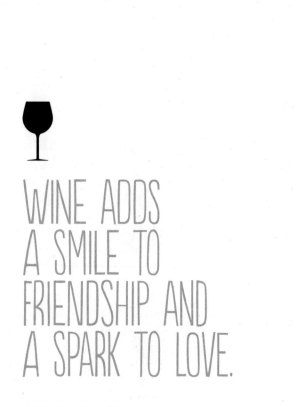

WINE ADDS
A SMILE TO
FRIENDSHIP AND
A SPARK TO LOVE.

EDMONDO DE AMICIS

CHAMPAGNE!
IN VICTORY ONE
DESERVES IT;
IN DEFEAT ONE
NEEDS IT.

NAPOLEON BONAPARTE

WHEN
I DRINK,
I THINK;
AND WHEN
I THINK,
I DRINK.

FRANCOIS
RABELAIS

I ENJOY LONG
ROMANTIC WALKS
DOWN THE
WINE AISLE.

ANONYMOUS

WINE AND
FRIENDS ARE A
great blend.

ERNEST HEMINGWAY

GIVE ME WINE TO

WASH ME CLEAN OF

THE WEATHER-STAINS

OF CARES.

RALPH WALDO EMERSON

ALCOHOL

— *may not* —

SOLVE YOUR

problems,

BUT NEITHER

will water

OR MILK.

ANONYMOUS

A BOTTLE
OF WINE BEGS
TO BE SHARED;
I HAVE NEVER
MET A MISERLY
WINE LOVER.

CLIFTON FADIMAN

GOOD WINE IS A
GOOD FAMILIAR
CREATURE IF IT
BE WELL USED.

WILLIAM SHAKESPEARE

THE CHURCH IS NEAR,
BUT THE ROAD IS ICY.
THE BAR IS FAR AWAY, BUT
I WILL WALK CAREFULLY.

RUSSIAN PROVERB

FROM WINE
WHAT SUDDEN
FRIENDSHIP SPRINGS!

JOHN GAY

WINE CHEERS THE SAD,
REVIVES THE OLD, INSPIRES
THE YOUNG, MAKES WEARINESS
FORGET HIS TOIL.

LORD BYRON

A MEAL
WITHOUT WINE
IS LIKE A
DAY WITHOUT
SUNSHINE.

JEAN ANTHELME BRILLAT-SAVAR

ON SOME DAYS,
MY HEAD IS FILLED WITH SUCH
WILD AND ORIGINAL THOUGHTS
THAT I CAN BARELY UTTER A
WORD. ON OTHER DAYS, THE
LIQUOR STORE IS CLOSED.

FRANK VARANO

WHEN I READ ABOUT THE EVILS OF DRINKING, I GAVE UP READING.

HENNY YOUNGMAN

I ONLY DRINK
CHAMPAGNE ON TWO
OCCASIONS. WHEN
I AM IN LOVE AND
WHEN I AM NOT.

COCO CHANEL

IN WINE THERE IS
WISDOM, IN BEER THERE
IS FREEDOM, IN WATER
THERE IS BACTERIA.

DAVID AUERBACH

THE SHARPER IS THE BERRY, THE SWEETER IS THE WINE.

PROVERB

JUST THE
SIMPLE ACT
OF TASTING A
GLASS OF WINE
IS ITS OWN
EVENT.

DAVID HYDE PIERCE

WINE TO ME IS PASSION... WINE IS ART. IT'S CULTURE. IT'S THE ESSENCE OF CIVILISATION AND THE ART OF LIVING.

ROBERT MONDAVI

IF THIS DOG DO YOU
BITE, SOON AS OUT
OF YOUR BED, TAKE
A HAIR OF THE TAIL
IN THE MORNING.

SCOTTISH PROVERB

GOOD WINE
PRAISES
ITSELF.

DUTCH PROVERB

DRINK
WINE, NOT
LABELS.

MAYNARD
AMERINE

ALCOHOL, TAKEN
IN SUFFICIENT
QUANTITIES, MAY
PRODUCE ALL
THE EFFECTS OF
DRUNKENNESS.

OSCAR WILDE

SOBER OR
BLOTTO, THIS IS
YOUR MOTTO:

keep muddling

through.

P. G. WODEHOUSE

BURGUNDY MAKES YOU

THINK OF SILLY THINGS,

BORDEAUX MAKES YOU

TALK OF THEM AND

CHAMPAGNE MAKES

YOU DO THEM.

JEAN ANTHELME BRILLAT-SAVARIN

WHEN A
—*recipe says*—
'ADD WINE',
never ask
'TO WHAT?'

ANONYMOUS

ALL WINES SHOULD
BE TASTED; SOME
SHOULD ONLY BE
SIPPED, BUT WITH
OTHERS, DRINK THE
WHOLE BOTTLE.

PAULO COELHO

MEET ME DOWN
IN THE BAR! WE'LL
DRINK BREAKFAST
TOGETHER.

W. C. FIELDS

DRINK WINE, AND YOU WILL
SLEEP WELL. SLEEP, AND YOU
WILL NOT SIN. AVOID SIN, AND
YOU WILL BE SAVED. ERGO,
DRINK WINE AND BE SAVED.

MEDIEVAL GERMAN PROVERB

RED WINE IS JUST
LIKE KETCHUP: IT GOES
WITH EVERYTHING.

JASON WALTON

A DRINK A DAY KEEPS

THE SHRINK AWAY.

EDWARD ABBEY

THE FLAVOUR
OF WINE IS
LIKE DELICATE
POETRY.

LOUIS PASTEUR

SOMETIMES
TOO MUCH TO DRINK
IS BARELY ENOUGH.

MARK TWAIN

AGE AND GLASSES OF WINE SHOULD NEVER BE COUNTED.

ITALIAN PROVERB

WINE IS THE THINKING PERSON'S HEALTH DRINK.

PHILLIP NORRIE

I DRINK WHEN I HAVE
OCCASION, AND
SOMETIMES WHEN I
HAVE NO OCCASION.

MIGUEL DE CERVANTES

PENICILLIN CURES,
BUT WINE MAKES
PEOPLE HAPPY.

ALEXANDER FLEMING

IF FOOD IS
THE BODY OF
GOOD LIVING,
WINE IS ITS
SOUL.

CLIFTON FADIMAN

THE JUICE OF THE GRAPE IS THE LIQUID QUINTESSENCE OF CONCENTRATED SUNBEAMS.

THOMAS LOVE PEACOCK

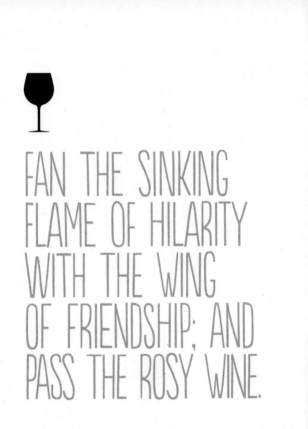

FAN THE SINKING FLAME OF HILARITY WITH THE WING OF FRIENDSHIP; AND PASS THE ROSY WINE.

CHARLES DICKENS

WHEN A MAN DRINKS WINE AT DINNER, HE BEGINS TO BE BETTER PLEASED WITH HIMSELF.

PLATO

REALITY IS
AN ILLUSION
CREATED BY
A LACK OF
ALCOHOL.

N. F. SIMPSON

WINE IS A
LIVING LIQUID
CONTAINING NO
PRESERVATIVES.

JULIA CHILD

I NEVER
TRUST A MAN
THAT DOESN'T

drink.

JOHN WAYNE

LET SCHOOLMASTERS

PUZZLE THEIR BRAIN,

WITH GRAMMAR, AND

NONSENSE, AND LEARNING,

GOOD LIQUOR,

I STOUTLY MAINTAIN,

GIVES GENIUS A

BETTER DISCERNING.

OLIVER GOLDSMITH

I RATHER
— *like* —
BAD WINE;
one gets
SO BORED
with
GOOD WINE.

BENJAMIN DISRAELI

MY ONLY
REGRET IS THAT I
HAVE NOT DRUNK
MORE CHAMPAGNE
IN MY LIFE.

JOHN MAYNARD KEYNES
ON HIS DEATHBED

THE WORSE YOU
ARE AT THINKING,
THE BETTER YOU
ARE AT DRINKING.

TERRY GOODKIND

WINE MAKES DAILY
LIVING EASIER, LESS HURRIED,
WITH FEWER TENSIONS AND
MORE TOLERANCE.

BENJAMIN FRANKLIN

WINE REJOICES THE
HEART OF MAN AND
JOY IS THE MOTHER
OF ALL VIRTUES.

JOHANN WOLFGANG VON GOETHE

I HAVE LIVED TEMPERATELY...
I DOUBLE THE DOCTOR'S
RECOMMENDATION OF A
GLASS AND A HALF OF
WINE EACH DAY AND EVEN
TREBLE IT WITH A FRIEND.

THOMAS JEFFERSON

THE GREAT EVIL
OF WINE IS THAT
IT FIRST SEIZES
THE FEET, IT
IS A CRAFTY
WRESTLER.

TITUS MACCIUS PLAUTUS

I NEVER

TASTE THE WINE FIRST
IN RESTAURANTS, I
JUST ASK THE WAITER
TO POUR.

NIGELLA LAWSON

WINE IS
PERHAPS THE
CLOSEST THING
THE PLANET
HAS TO AN
ELIXIR OF LIFE.

WINE BRINGS TO
LIGHT THE HIDDEN
SECRETS OF
THE SOUL.

HORACE

WINE MAKES A
MAN MORE PLEASED
WITH HIMSELF; I DO
NOT SAY THAT IT
MAKES HIM MORE
PLEASING TO OTHERS.

SAMUEL JOHNSON

BUT I'M NOT SO
THINK AS YOU
DRUNK I AM.

J. C. SQUIRE

THE BEST WINES
ARE THE ONES
WE DRINK WITH
FRIENDS.

ANONYMOUS

THE DISCOVERY OF A GOOD WINE IS INCREASINGLY BETTER FOR MANKIND THAN THE DISCOVERY OF A NEW STAR.

LEONARDO DA VINCI

DRINK IS THE
FEAST OF REASON
AND THE FLOW
OF SOUL.

ALEXANDER POPE

EITHER GIVE
ME MORE WINE
OR LEAVE
ME ALONE.

RUMI

A GOURMET
MEAL
WITHOUT
A GLASS
OF WINE
JUST SEEMS
TRAGIC
TO ME
SOMEHOW.

KATHY MATTEA

WINE IS MORE
THAN A BEVERAGE,
IT'S A LIFESTYLE.

ANONYMOUS

THE PROBLEM
WITH THE
WORLD IS THAT
EVERYONE IS

a few

drinks

BEHIND.

HUMPHREY BOGART

I HAVE TAKEN MORE

OUT OF ALCOHOL

THAN ALCOHOL HAS

TAKEN OUT OF ME.

WINSTON CHURCHILL

THREE

— *be the* —

THINGS I SHALL

never attain:

ENVY, CONTENT,

and sufficient

CHAMPAGNE.

DOROTHY PARKER

I KNEW I WAS
DRUNK. I FELT
SOPHISTICATED
AND COULDN'T
PRONOUNCE IT.

ANONYMOUS

CANDY
IS DANDY
BUT LIQUOR
IS QUICKER.

OGDEN NASH

NOTHING MAKES THE FUTURE
LOOK SO ROSY AS TO
CONTEMPLATE IT THROUGH A
GLASS OF CHAMBERTIN.

NAPOLEON BONAPARTE

WINE... THE
INTELLECTUAL PART
OF THE MEAL.

ALEXANDRE DUMAS

HE WHO LOVES NOT WINE,
WOMEN AND SONG REMAINS A
FOOL HIS WHOLE LIFE LONG.

MARTIN LUTHER

WINE, TAKEN
IN MODERATION,
MAKES LIFE, FOR A
MOMENT, BETTER,
AND WHEN THE
MOMENT PASSES
LIFE DOES NOT
FOR THAT REASON
BECOME WORSE.

BERNARD LEVIN

WINE

FILLS THE HEART
WITH COURAGE.

PLATO

AWAY WITH YOU, WATER, DESTRUCTION OF WINE!

CATULLUS

IF WE SIP THE WINE, WE
FIND DREAMS COMING
UPON US OUT OF THE
IMMINENT NIGHT.

D. H. LAWRENCE

QUICKLY, BRING ME
A BEAKER OF WINE,
SO THAT I MAY WET
MY MIND AND SAY
SOMETHING CLEVER.

ARISTOPHANES

FOR WHEN THE WINE IS IN, THE WIT IS OUT.

THOMAS BECON

GOOD
COMPANY, GOOD
WINE, GOOD
WELCOME, CAN
MAKE GOOD
PEOPLE.

WILLIAM SHAKESPEARE

ABSTAINER: A WEAK PERSON WHO YIELDS TO THE TEMPTATION OF DENYING HIMSELF A PLEASURE.

AMBROSE BIERCE

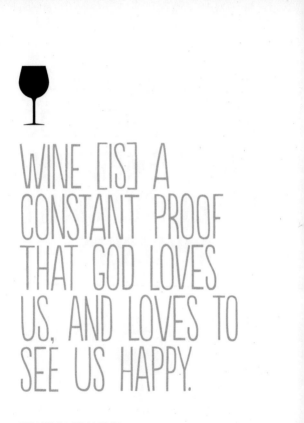

WINE [IS] A CONSTANT PROOF THAT GOD LOVES US, AND LOVES TO SEE US HAPPY.

BENJAMIN FRANKLIN

COME QUICKLY,
I AM DRINKING
THE STARS!

DOM PÉRIGNON

GREAT WINE
WORKS
WONDERS
AND IS
ITSELF ONE.

EDWARD
STEINBERG

WINE IS JUST A
CONVERSATION
WAITING TO
HAPPEN.

JESSICA ALTIERI

GIVE ME A BOWL
OF WINE. IN THIS
I BURY ALL

unkindness.

WILLIAM SHAKESPEARE

ONE NOT ONLY DRINKS

THE WINE, ONE SMELLS IT,

OBSERVES IT, TASTES IT,

SIPS IT, AND – ONE

TALKS ABOUT IT.

EDWARD VII

A BOTTLE
— *of good* —
WINE, LIKE
a good act,
SHINES EVER
in the
RETROSPECT.

ROBERT LOUIS STEVENSON

THE CONNOISSEUR
DOES NOT DRINK
WINE BUT TASTES
OF ITS SECRETS.

SALVADOR DALÍ

WINE IS THE
MOST HEALTHFUL
AND MOST HYGIENIC
OF BEVERAGES.

LOUIS PASTEUR

CHAMPAGNE IS THE
ONLY WINE THAT LEAVES
A WOMAN BEAUTIFUL
AFTER DRINKING IT.

MADAME DE POMPADOUR

WHERE THERE IS
NO WINE THERE
IS NO LOVE.

EURIPIDES

WINE IS EARTH'S ANSWER
TO THE SUN.

MARGARET FULLER

TO HAPPY
CONVENTS,
BOSOMED DEEP
IN VINES, WHERE
SLUMBER ABBOTS,
PURPLE AS
THEIR WINES.

ALEXANDER POPE

DRINKING

IS A WAY OF
ENDING THE DAY.

ERNEST HEMINGWAY

HEALTH — WHAT MY FRIENDS ARE ALWAYS DRINKING TO BEFORE THEY FALL DOWN.

PHYLLIS DILLER

THERE IS A
COMMUNION OF MORE
THAN OUR BODIES
WHEN BREAD IS BROKEN
AND WINE DRUNK.

M. F. K. FISHER

MAN, BEING
REASONABLE,
MUST GET DRUNK;
THE BEST OF LIFE IS
BUT INTOXICATION.

LORD BYRON

IN WINE THERE IS TRUTH.

PLINY THE ELDER

HIS LIPS DRINK
WATER, BUT HIS
HEART DRINKS
WINE.

E. E. CUMMINGS

WITHIN THE BOTTLE'S DEPTHS, THE WINE'S SOUL SANG ONE NIGHT.

CHARLES BAUDELAIRE

POUR YOURSELF
A DRINK, PUT ON
SOME LIPSTICK AND
PULL YOURSELF
TOGETHER.

ELIZABETH TAYLOR

MAY OUR LOVE
BE LIKE GOOD
WINE; GROW
STRONGER AS IT
GROWS OLDER.

OLD ENGLISH TOAST

WITHOUT
BREAD
AND WINE,
LOVE GOES
HUNGRY.

LATIN PROVERB

THE WINE-CUP
IS THE LITTLE
SILVER WELL,
WHERE TRUTH, IF
TRUTH THERE BE,
DOTH DWELL.

WILLIAM SHAKESPEARE

GOOD WINE IS
a necessity
of life
FOR ME.

THOMAS JEFFERSON

THERE IS NOT THE
HUNDREDTH PART OF THE
WINE CONSUMED IN THIS
KINGDOM THAT THERE
OUGHT TO BE.

OUR FOGGY CLIMATE

WANTS HELP.

JANE AUSTEN

TOO MUCH OF
— *anything* —
IS BAD, BUT
too much
CHAMPAGNE
is just
RIGHT.

F. SCOTT FITZGERALD

TO TAKE WINE
INTO OUR MOUTHS
IS TO SAVOUR
A DROPLET OF
THE RIVER OF
HUMAN HISTORY.

CLIFTON FADIMAN

WINE CAN BE
A BETTER TEACHER
THAN INK.

STEPHEN FRY

WE ARE ALL MORTAL UNTIL
THE FIRST KISS AND THE
SECOND GLASS OF WINE.

EDUARDO GALEANO

SIP,

SWIRL,

SWALLOW.

ANONYMOUS

BURGUNDY FOR KINGS,

CHAMPAGNE FOR DUCHESSES,

CLARET FOR GENTLEMEN.

FRENCH PROVERB

ALCOHOL IS A
MISUNDERSTOOD
VITAMIN.

P. G. WODEHOUSE

BE CAREFUL

TO TRUST A PERSON

WHO DOES NOT LIKE WINE.

KARL MARX

WOMAN FIRST TEMPTED MAN TO EAT; HE TOOK TO DRINKING OF HIS OWN ACCORD.

JOHN R. KEMBLE

WINE IS THE INCARNATION - IT IS BOTH DIVINE AND HUMAN.

PAUL TILLICH

I FEEL SORRY FOR
PEOPLE WHO DON'T
DRINK. WHEN THEY
WAKE UP IN THE
MORNING, THAT'S AS
GOOD AS THEY'RE
GOING TO FEEL ALL DAY.

FRANK SINATRA

WINE IS SUNLIGHT, HELD TOGETHER BY WATER.

GALILEO

WITH BREAD
AND WINE YOU
CAN WALK
YOUR ROAD.

SPANISH PROVERB

THIS IS ONE OF THE DISADVANTAGES OF WINE; IT MAKES A MAN MISTAKE WORDS FOR THOUGHTS.

SAMUEL JOHNSON

WINE MAKES EVERY
MEAL AN OCCASION,
EVERY TABLE MORE
ELEGANT, EVERY DAY
MORE CIVILISED.

ANDRE SIMON

WINE CAN OF
THEIR WITS THE
WISE BEGUILE,
MAKE THE SAGE
FROLIC AND THE
SERIOUS SMILE.

HOMER

WHAT'S
DRINKING?
A MERE
PAUSE FROM
THINKING!

LORD BYRON

THERE COMES A
TIME IN EVERY
WOMAN'S LIFE
WHEN THE ONLY
THING THAT HELPS
IS A GLASS OF
CHAMPAGNE.

BETTE DAVIS

GIVE ME BOOKS,

French wine,

FRUIT, FINE
WEATHER AND
A LITTLE MUSIC
PLAYED OUT
OF DOORS...

JOHN KEATS

WINE GIVES MAN

NOTHING... IT ONLY

PUTS IN MOTION WHAT

HAD BEEN LOCKED

UP IN FROST.

SAMUEL JOHNSON

WINE

— *is* —

INSPIRING

and adds

GREATLY

to the

JOY OF LIVING.

NAPOLEON BONAPARTE

HERE'S TO
ALCOHOL, THE
ROSE-COLOURED
GLASSES OF LIFE.

F. SCOTT FITZGERALD

If you're interested in finding
out more about our books,
find us on Facebook at
Summersdale Publishers
and follow us on Twitter
at **@ Summersdale**.

www.summersdale.com